LOOK AT WHAT'S INSIDE...

Blippi™

There is so much **to do inside!**

THIS BRILLIANT **BLIPPI** ANNUAL BELONGS TO

....

TURN THE PAGE TO START THE FUN...

LittleBrother BOOKS

Published 2022.
Little Brother Books Ltd, Ground Floor,
23 Southernhay East, Exeter, Devon EX1 1QL
books@littlebrotherbooks.co.uk | www.littlebrotherbooks.co.uk
Printed in China. Xuantan Temple Industrial Zone,
Gulao Town, Heshan, Guangdong.

MEET Blippi™

Hey, it's me, Blippi, and these pages are all about me! Awesome!

Hello **friend!**

Blippi has 6 letters.
Can you circle the number 6?

2   4   6

Answers on pages 76-77.

My name begins with the letter B.
Tick the fruit that also begins with a b.

These are some of my favourite things. Draw lines to match each word to the right picture.

Painting

Animals

Music

I love ice cream. Can you colour this ice cream for me to eat? Yum!

My best friend is Meekah. Trace over the letters to write her name.

Meekah

ZOOM TO THE MOON

5, 4, 3, 2, 1 **blast off!!**

I'm blasting into space to see my friend, Rocky the moon rock. Can you help me avoid the planets on the way?

START

FINISH

1, 2, 3 COUNT WITH Blippi™

> Let's learn **together!**

Counting is so much fun! Can you count with me, then write the numbers?

1 rainbow

2 dinosaurs

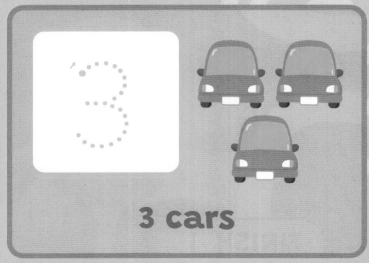

3 cars

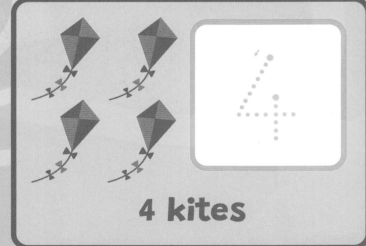

4 kites

5 trees

6 apples

7 balloons

8 ice creams

9 presents

10 flowers

FUN ON THE FARM

Hey, it's me, Farmer Blippi! I've lost some of my animals – can you spot them hiding in the picture below?

OVER TO YOU!

You know lots about me, now I'd like to find out about you! Fill in these pages all about yourself.

My name is:

_____

I am
3v
_____
year's old.

Draw a picture of yourself with me!

W

14

My favourite colour is:

Colour the paint splat your favourite colour.

My favourite food is:

Draw your favourite food here.

You sound **amazing!**

I love:
Dancing
Singing
Painting
Climbing

SPOT IT!

Can you spot the patterns below and work out what colours the white pictures should be? Let's go!

Colour the last picture the right **colour!**

1

2

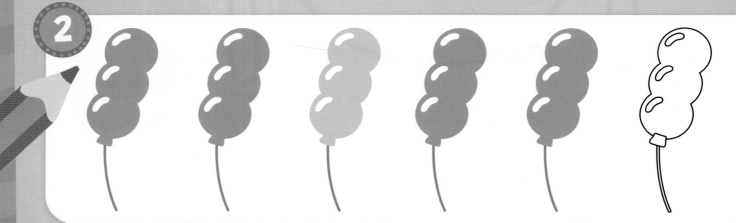

3

Answers on pages 76-77.

LEARN WITH Blippi™

There's lots to learn about letters so let's get started!

Write your name here. Can you find the letters in the alphabet below?

My favorite letter is M for **Meekah!**

Colour your favourite letter.

ABCDEFGHIJKLM
NOPQRSTUVWXYZ

There are 26 letters in the alphabet.

Which letter do all of these things begin with?

MEOW!

BEEP! BEEP!

Circle the animal that begins with the letter m.

Trace over the letters to finish the words.

kite

sun

My favorite letter is B for **Blippi!**

tree

Answers on pages 76-77.

MINI MONSTERS

These roar-some monster finger puppets are easy to make and fun to play with too!

Ask an adult to help.

YOU WILL NEED

- A few egg boxes
- Scissors
- Colourful paint
- A paintbrush
- Coloured paper
- Googly eyes
- Glue
- A black marker pen

Follow the trail the happy monster has made.

Wow! Look at this!

1 Carefully cut out the cone shaped pieces from inside an egg box. Each piece will make one finger puppet monster.

2 Paint your cones with bright colours.

3

Cut two strips of coloured paper (about 10cm by 0.5cm) for each monster. Glue the strips onto the top of the cone and either concertina fold them or curl them with scissors.

4

Glue a googly eye onto each monster and use a black marker pen to draw on a mouth. Your mini monsters are now ready to roar!

Blippi's™ BUSY DAY

Today I'm working on a building site. Join in the fun by completing the activities along the trail.

Check out my **hard hat!**

START

1

I'm ready to start work but I need one more tool. Trace over the letters to see which one.

hammer

2

Count how many cones I've put out.

Answers on pages 76-77.

3 Tick which vehicle will help me dig a big hole.

4 Lunch break! Add a refreshing drink in the glass to go with my yummy food.

5 I need to put a barrier in front of the hole so nobody falls in. Circle the biggest barrier.

a

b

c

Now it's **hometime!**

FINISH

23

HOW DO YOU FEEL?

I'm feeling **happy!**

Most of the time I feel happy, but sometimes I feel sad or tired or grumpy. Help me complete these activities all about different feelings.

Trace over the words to see how T.A.B.B.S. is feeling in each of these pictures.

happy

sad

D.BO

Does D.BO look worried or excited?

worried   excited

24

I feel happy when I'm with my friends. Draw a picture of something that makes you happy.

I FEEL...

Use this chart to record your feelings over a week. Look at the pictures in the key and copy the one that best describes how you're feeling each morning, afternoon and evening.

Your feelings can be different **everyday!**

KEY

 happy   sad   excited   tired   worried

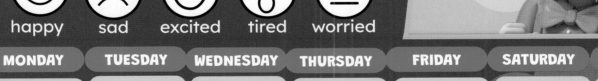

	MONDAY	TUESDAY	WEDNESDAY	THURSDAY	FRIDAY	SATURDAY	SUNDAY
MORNING							
AFTERNOON							
EVENING							

TRUE OR FALSE?

Let's **go!**

Read the descriptions of my friends then colour a tick or a cross to say whether they're true or false.

Sherry Pop the ice lolly has a strawberry on her head.

TRUE ✓ ✗ FALSE

Spencer the spider has blue hair.

TRUE ✓ ✗ FALSE

Bijon the bee has wings.

TRUE ✓ ✗ FALSE

Answers on pages 76-77.

3 IN A ROW

Are you ready for some fruity fun? Circle the fruit when you spot three in a row. Let's go!

Which fruit does a monkey like to eat?

banana

Answers on pages 76-77.

27

MOVE IT!

This action game is so much fun. Grab a friend or two and get moving!

YOU WILL NEED

- Scissors
- Glue or double-sided sticky tape

HOW TO MAKE

1. Cut out the template on the opposite page.
2. Fold along the lines to make a dice shape.
3. Add glue or double-sided sticky tape to the tabs and stick your dice together.

HOW TO PLAY

1. Take it in turns to roll the dice.
2. Copy the action that the dice lands on.
3. Keep playing for as long as you like!

Ask an adult to help.

Do a funny dance!

Wave at a friend!

Run as fast as you can!

Look up and down!

Squat down and raise your arms.

Swing your arms to the right and left.

Make sure you read page 30 before you cut out the dice template. If you don't want to cut up your book, photocopy or scan and print this page instead.

SHAPE SPOTTING

Shapes are everywhere! Let's check some of them out.

1 Trace over the dotted lines to draw the shapes.

Circle **Triangle** **Rectangle** **Square**

2 My lunch is lots of different shapes. Draw lines to match each piece of food to the right shape.

Circle **Square** **Triangle** **Semi-circle**

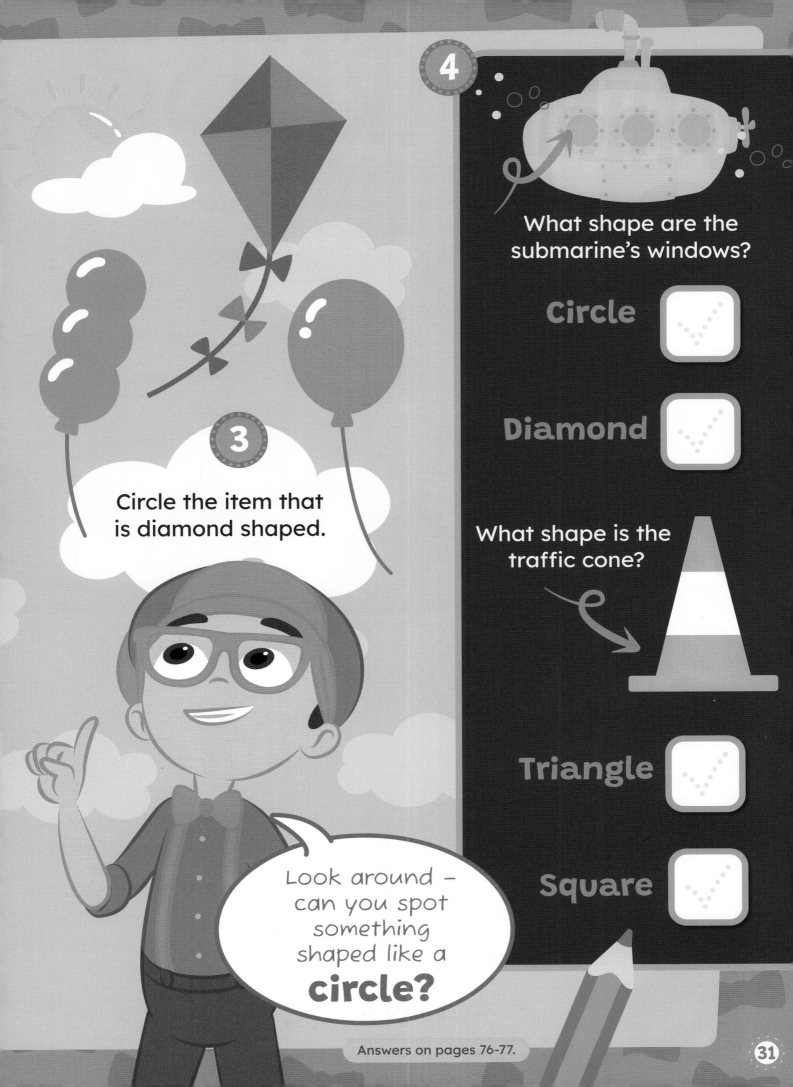

What shape are the submarine's windows?

Circle

Diamond

What shape is the traffic cone?

Triangle

Square

③ Circle the item that is diamond shaped.

④

Look around – can you spot something shaped like a **circle?**

Answers on pages 76-77.

ANIMAL TRAILS

These animals are on the move!
Follow the trails they've made with
your finger or a pencil.

Wow!
Look at that!

Draw a trail for the galloping horse.

HISS!

HISS!

The snake is slithering.

BOING!

BOING!

Here comes the hopping bunny.

OOH!

OOH!

Follow the swinging monkey.

33

LET'S EXPLORE

Diggers are used to dig holes in the ground. Let's find out more...

The bucket scoops up the soil or rubble.

Which close up isn't from the digger?

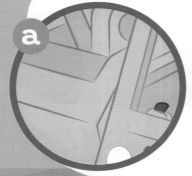

a

b

c

The long arm moves and bends. It's controlled by the driver.

What colour is the digger?

a

b

Let's get **digging!**

What else can be used to dig a hole? Circle your answer.

a

b

Tracks help the digger stay stable on uneven ground.

Answers on pages 76-77.

35

PICTURE PUZZLE

Look **Closely!**

The pictures below may look the same but they're not. That's sneaky! Circle the right picture to answer each question.

1 Which two shoes make a matching pair?

a   b   c   d

2 Which cute fox is the smallest?

a   b   c

3 Which colourful paint palette is the odd one out?

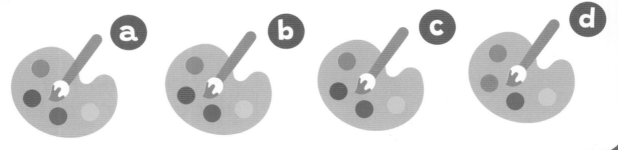

a   b   c   d

FAMILY FUN

Trace over the dotted line to finish the picture of this happy bear family. Sooooo cute!

How many bear cubs can you **count?**

Can you spot this flower somewhere on the page? Tick the box when you've found it.

Blippi VISITS A CHOCOLATE FACTORY

I love chocolate! Do you?
But how is a chocolate bar made?
Let's find the answer to my question.

1

Here I am outside the chocolate factory. Let's go inside and find out more.

2

Check it out! This friendly chocolate bar is going to give me a tour!

3

Meet the cocoa beans. They come from plants and are the most important ingredient.

4

First the beans have a bath to get nice and clean. That looks fun!

I just eat a bit of chocolate, not **too much!**

Circle your favourite kind of chocolate.

5

Then they get roasty and toasty and are made into bean powder. Cool!

6

The bean powder is mixed with sugar and milk to make it sweet and smooth. Sounds good!

7

Then the chocolate is cooled into bar shapes and wrapped. Now it's ready to eat. Yum!

8

And now I have the answer to my question. Upload answer D.BO!

THE END

HANDPRINT ART

Here's how to make an awesome jellyfish picture using your handprint. Super messy fun!

Check this out!

Ask an adult to help.

YOU WILL NEED

- Colourful paint
- A paintbrush
- Googly eyes
- Glue
- Black marker pen

HOW TO MAKE

1. Ask your grown-up to cut out the underwater scene on the opposite page.

2. Use a paintbrush to cover one of your hands in paint, then make a handprint on the scene.

3. Wash your hand, then cover it with a different colour paint and make another handprint on the scene. Leave the paint to dry.

4. Stick googly eyes on your handprint jellyfish and draw on smiles with a black marker pen.

5. Hang your jellyfish picture up for everyone to see.

Make sure you read page 42 before you cut your underwater picture out. If you don't want to cut up your book, photocopy or scan and print page 41 instead.

41

RAINBOW COLOURS

If you mix two colours together, you make a new colour. Let's learn together.

Colour the white paint splats the right colours.

Use the original colours and the new colours you've made to colour this bunch of balloons.

Answers on pages 76-77.

HEALTHY EATING

We need a balanced diet to keep our bodies healthy. Let's find out more.

There are five main food groups.

1 VEGETABLES

2 FRUIT

3 BREAD, CEREALS AND PASTA

4 MEAT, FISH AND EGGS

5 MILK AND CHEESE

Try and eat something from each food group **everyday!**

egg sandwich carrot cheese cherries

Which food group do each of these foods belong to?

Draw yourself a healthy dinner.

Don't forget to draw a drink!

Now, choose a yummy pudding.

If you have a healthy diet, it's OK to have a treat **sometimes!**

Answers on pages 76-77.

45

ALL ABOARD!

Get **spotting!**

The BlippiMobile is ready for adventure! Can you spot six differences between these two pictures?

Colour a number each time you spot a difference.

1 2 3 4 5 6

Which attachment is the BlippiMobile using?

a

duck feet

b

Wings

Which of these creatures has wings?

a **b**

Answers on pages 76-77.

UNDER THE SEA

Ready, set, **explore!**

The BlippiMobile is ready for adventure! Join me in the ocean for some underwater fun.

1

What should I activate on the BlippiMobile to go underwater?

a

snorkel

b

wings

2

Jerry the jellyfish has been swimming all around the ocean. Trace the trail he's made along the way.

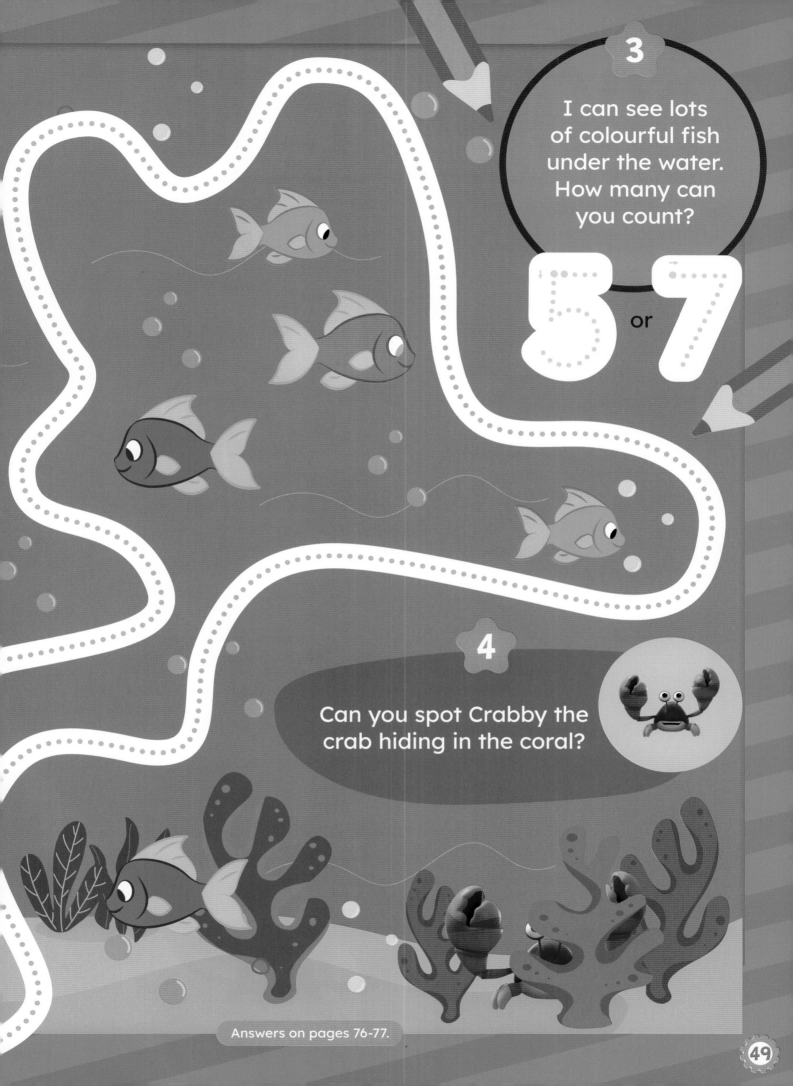

3

I can see lots of colourful fish under the water. How many can you count?

5 or 7

4

Can you spot Crabby the crab hiding in the coral?

Answers on pages 76-77.

DOODLE TIME

Hello, I'm at the beach. Follow the instructions to finish this sandy scene.

Draw some fish swimming in the sea.

Doodle an ice cream in my hand.

Doodle some sunglasses for Crabby to wear.

Add a shining sun in the sky.

Add some flags on top of the sandcastle.

Draw a sunhat on T.A.B.B.S.' head.

51

PICTURE CROSSWORD

Use the pictures to help you fill in this crossword. All the words are things you'll find growing outdoors.

ON THE MOVE

Circle the vehicles that match the shadows

Look at all these awesome vehicles. Can you match each shadow to the correct one? It's going to be fun!

1

a digger

b boat

2

a car

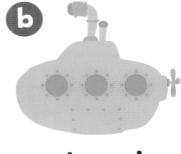
b submarine

3

a train

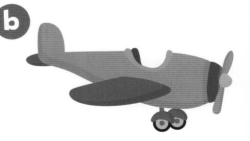
b plane

Answers on pages 76-77.

FUN WITH OPPOSITES

These words are all opposites. Can you choose the right word for each picture? Let's go!

1

The ice cream I'm eating is... **hot** **cold**

2

Is the monster truck big or small? **big** **small**

3

Do I look happy or sad? **happy** **sad**

4

The bird Meekah's watching is flying... **high** **low**

5

Is my umbrella open or closed?

 open   closed

6

Am I inside or outside the tractor?

 inside   outside

7

My end of the seesaw is...

 up   down

8

Am I above or below the water?

 above   below

Colour this star when you have **finished!**

OUT AND ABOUT

Ask an adult to help.

Look, I'm in the countryside. Join in the fun by cutting out the pictures opposite and sticking them on the scene.

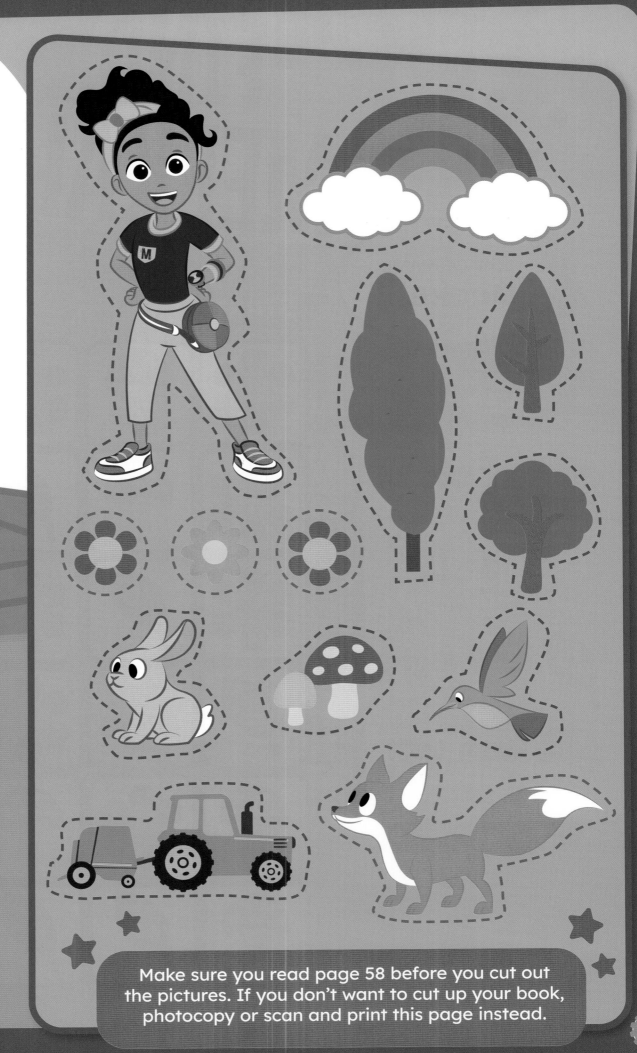

Make sure you read page 58 before you cut out the pictures. If you don't want to cut up your book, photocopy or scan and print this page instead.

57

FIND MEEKAH

I'm coming, **Meekah!**

START

KEY

Down

Up

Right

Left

I can hear Meekah calling me but I can't see her. Can you use the key below to lead me to her?

I'm here, **Blippi!**

FINISH

Answers on pages 76-77.

PAPER PLATE BUNNY

Make your own super cute bunny from a paper plate. So much fun!

Ask an adult to help.

YOU WILL NEED

- Paper plate
- White, pink and blue A4 paper
- Scissors
- Glue
- White pipe cleaner x 2
- A black marker pen

1

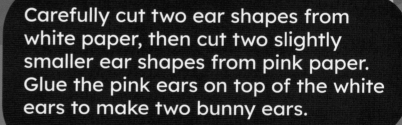

Carefully cut two ear shapes from white paper, then cut two slightly smaller ear shapes from pink paper. Glue the pink ears on top of the white ears to make two bunny ears.

2

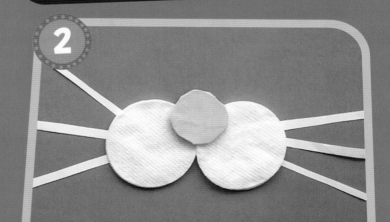

Cut out two circles from white paper and a smaller circle from pink paper. Then cut each pipe cleaner into three. Glue the circles together to make the bunny's cheeks and nose, then glue the pipe cleaner pieces either side of the cheeks to make whiskers.

Answers on pages 76-77.

3

Cut two eye shapes from blue paper and two small circles from white paper. Glue the circles onto the blue eye shapes, then draw on pupils with a black marker pen.

4

Glue the ears, eyes and nose onto a paper plate and your bunny friend is finished.

How many carrots can you **find?**

WOULD YOU RATHER...?

Tick the boxes to say which food you'd rather eat in this fun game!

Super silly **fun!**

OR

cheese

apple

OR

pizza

ice cream

OR

chocolate

strawberry

COLOUR BY NUMBERS

I love the smell of **flowers.**

Check this out! You can use the numbers to help you colour this flower. Let's try!

COLOUR KEY

DID YOU KNOW?

Flowers need sun and rain to help them grow.

DINO MATCH

I've gone back in time to when dinosaurs lived on Earth! That's so cool! Can you draw lines to match these cute baby dinos into pairs?

a

c

g

k

Great **matching!**

Answers on pages 76-77.

ALL ABOUT LIONS

Look out, there are lions about! Let's find out more about these big cats.

Fully grown male lions have a mane of hair around their head. Wow!

A baby lion is called a cub. Cute!

Check this **out!**

Answers on pages 76-77.

Trace over the letters to discover what noise a lion makes.

Roar

How many lion footprints can you count?

Most lions live in the African savannah.

A group of lions is called a pride.

Which tail belongs to a lion?

a

b

c

A COLOURFUL ADVENTURE

Read this story about how a rainbow gets its colours with your grown up. It's going to be fun!

One day, when I was out in the BlippiMobile with ,

it started to . Then the came out and a

colourful appeared in the sky. "I love s,"

I told , "I wonder how a  gets its colours?"

Then I had a brilliant idea. "We can fly up and ask

the  and find out."

First, I needed wings, so I activated the Blippi Station. Soon,

the BlippiMobile was ready for adventure and away we flew.

High up in the , I met Bowie the .

"Could you tell me how you get all of your colours?"

I asked. "Of course!" Bowie replied.

 T.A.B.B.S.
 rain
 sun
 rainbow
clouds

When you see a picture, say the word out loud.

Bowie explained that when it s there are lots of water droplets in the air. The droplets join together to make . "And when the shines through the water droplets in the , " Bowie said, "the light bends and separates into all the colours of the  ."

"That is awesome!" I cried. "I think I have the answer to my question." uploaded the answer and we flew back to the ground. "What a colouful adventure that was," I said happily.

Turn the page to answer questions about the story.

MEMORY TEST

Can you answer these questions about the story on the previous page? Let's go!

Tick the correct answers.

1
What came out after the rain stopped?

moon

sun

2
Who flew to the rainbow with me?

T.A.B.B.S

D.BO

3

What was the rainbow's name?

RAINY

BOWIE

4
What do water droplets make?

stars

clouds

RAINBOW RACE

Draw lines to connect the numbers in order from 1 to 10, to reach the rainbow. This is going to be fun!

7

1

3

2

8

4

9

6

5

10

Race you to the **rainbow!**

How many more raindrops do you need to draw to make 5?

ROCKET GAME

Let's **play!**

Will you be the first to colour your space rocket in this exciting game for two players? It's so much fun!

PLAYER 1

YOU WILL NEED:
• A dice
• Coloured pens

KEY

1 = Rocket body
2 = Round window
3 = Left fin
4 = Right fin
5 = Inner flame
6 = Outer flame

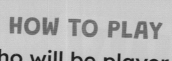

HOW TO PLAY

1. Decide who will be player 1 and who will be player 2.
2. Take it in turns to roll the dice, then look at the key and colour in the corresponding part of your rocket.
3. If you have already coloured in that part, pass the dice to the other player.
4. The first player to colour in all of their rocket is the winner.

PLAYER 2

Can you find the UFO hidden on these pages?

SNOWY ADVENTURE

Draw lines to match the missing pieces to the picture.

a

Brrr!

1

What should I be wearing to keep warm?

SUNGLASSES   COAT

Do you like playing in the snow?

YES   NO

74

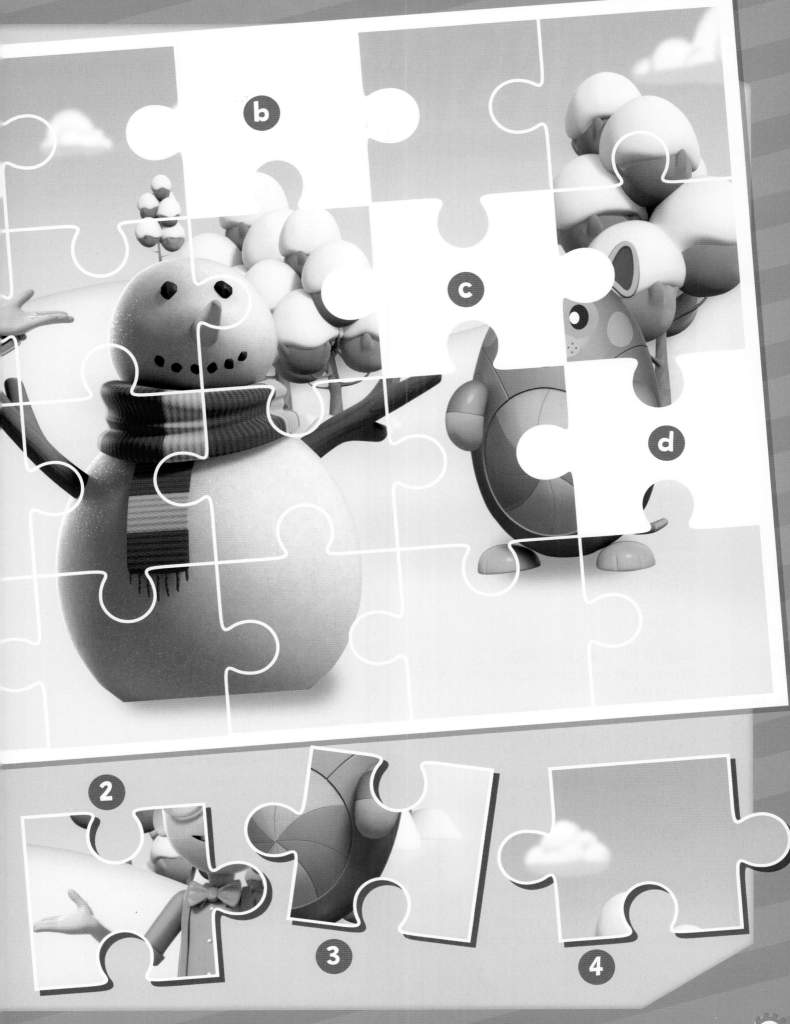

ANSWERS

Pages 6-7 –Meet Blippi
Banana begins with the letter b.

 Painting Animals Music

Pages 8-9 – Zoom to the Moon

Pages 12-13 – Fun on the Farm

Page 16 – Spot It!
1. Red Apple.
2. Yellow balloon.
3. Green tree.

Pages 18-19 – Learn with Blippi
Carrot, cat and car begin with the letter c.
Monkey begins with the letter m.

Pages 22-23 – Blippi's Busy Day
2. There are 6 cones.
3. The digger will help dig the hole.
5. b is the biggest barrier.

Pages 24-25 – How do you Feel?
D.BO looks worried.

Page 26 – True or False?
False – Sherry Pop has a blackberry on her head.
True – Spencer has blue hair.
True – Bijon has wings.

Page 27 – 3 in a Row

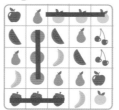

A monkey likes to eat a banana.

Pages 30-31 – Shape Spotting
2. Watermelon = semicircle, pizza = triangle, orange = circle, chocolate = square.
3. The kite is diamond shaped.
4. The Submarine's windows are circle shaped. The traffic cone is triangle shaped.

Pages 34-35 – Let's Explore
Close up b isn't from the digger.
The digger is yellow.
A spade can also be used to dig a hole.

Page 36 – Picture Puzzles
1. a and c.
2. c.
3. d.

Page 37 – Family Fun
There are 4 bear cubs.

Pages 42-43 – Rainbow Colours
Blue + yellow = green.
Yellow + red = orange.
Red + blue = purple.

Pages 44-45 – Healthy Eating
Egg – meat, fish and eggs.
Sandwich – bread, cereals and pasta.
Carrot – vegetables.
Chesse - milk and cheese.
Cherries - fruit.

Pages 46-47 - All Aboard!

The BlippiMobile is using wings.
The bee has wings.

Pages 48-49 - Under the Sea
1. Blippi should activate the snorkel.
3. There are 7 fish.
4.

Page 53 - On the Move
1. a.
2. b.
3. b.

Pages 54-55 - Fun with Opposites
1. Cold.
2. Big.
3. Happy.
4. High.
5. Open.
6. Inside.
7. Up.
8. Below.

Pages 58-59 - Find Meekah

Pages 60-61 - Paper Plate Bunny
There are 6 carrots.

Pages 64-65 - Dino Match
a and b, c and f, d and i, e and k,
g and j, h and l.

Pages 66-67 - All About Lions
There are 5 footprints.
Tail c belongs to a lion.

Page 70 - Memory Test
1. Sun.
2. T.A.B.B.S.
3. Bowie.
4. Clouds.

Page 71 - Rainbow Race

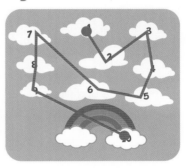

You need to draw 2 more
raindrops to make 5.

Pages 74-75 - Snowy Adventure
1 – c, 2 – a, 3 – d, 4 – b.
Blippi should be wearing a
coat to keep warm.